1ST GRADE PHONICS
Unit 7
Spelling More Syllable Types

TABLE OF CONTENTS

IMPORTANT: Please refer to the Teacher Guide for specific scripts, procedures, and words that are represented by pictures.

Throughout this Unit, learners will scan QR codes. Be careful they scan each code individually.

LEARN

- Spelling words with r-controlled syllables

- Spelling words with vowel teams **oy**, **ow**, and **oi**

- Spelling tricky words

DAILY PAGE GOALS

Day	Complete	Day	Complete	Day	Complete
1	ii–6	7	32–37	13	62–68
2	7–14	8	38–44	14	69–76
3	15–20	9	45–50	15	77–82
4	21–25	10	51–55	16	83–88
5	26–27	11	56–57	17	89–90
6	28–31	12	58–61	18	91–94

SKUNK 246

SKUNK

Teacher reads all pages to the learners.

Learn:

- Read and sort words with r-controlled vowels.

- Spell and read words from List 7.

WRITING PHONOGRAM REVIEW

**Listen to and write the phonograms.**
Underline any multi-letter phonograms.

WORKING WITH WORDS

Spelling List 7 has r-controlled vowels. The r-controlled vowels **er**, **ur**, and **ir** make the same sound. This can be tricky for spelling.

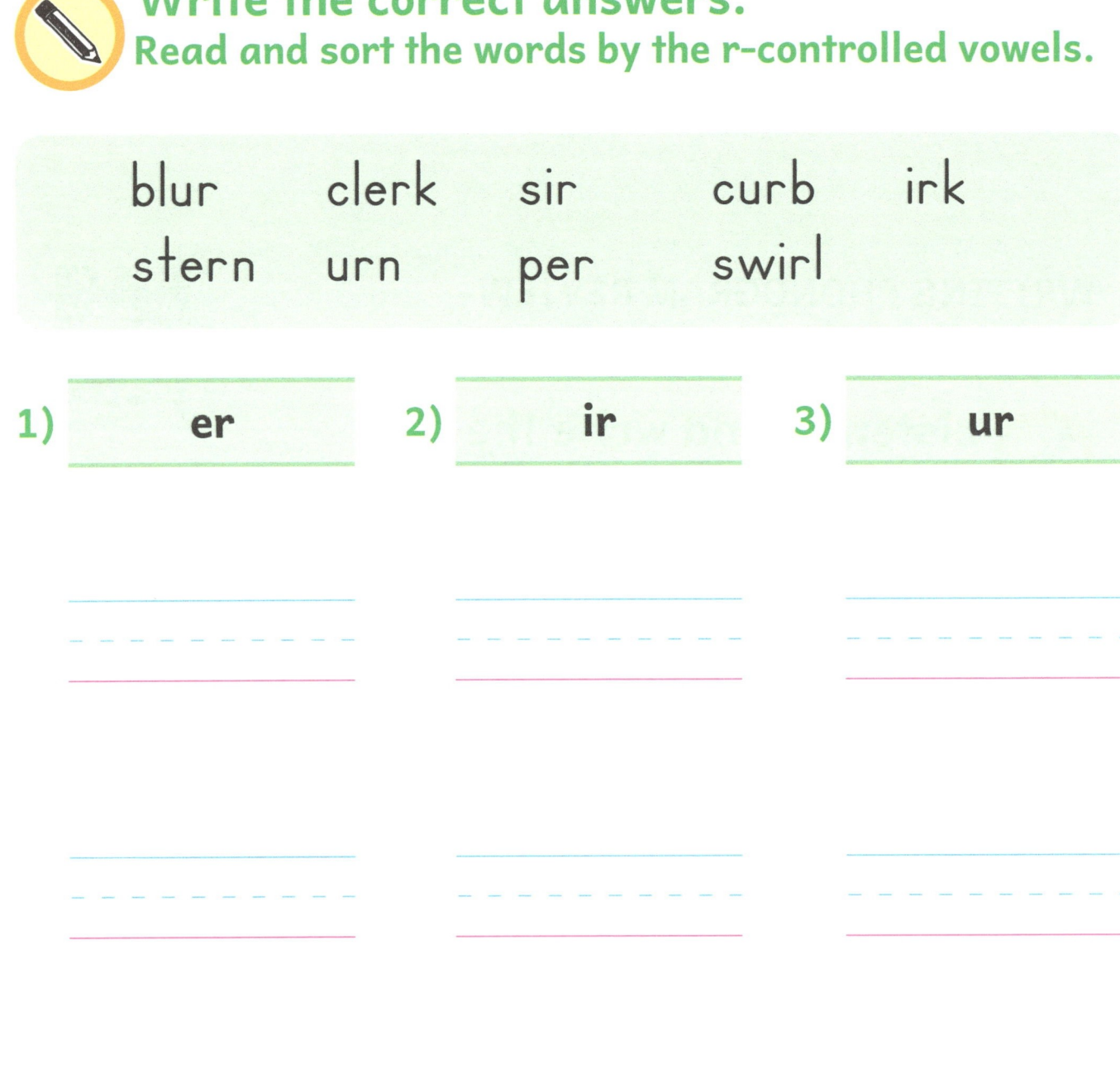

Write the correct answers.
Read and sort the words by the r-controlled vowels.

blur	clerk	sir	curb	irk
stern	urn	per	swirl	

1) **er**

2) **ir**

3) **ur**

Listen!

 **Circle the correct answers.**

| 4) | syllables | 1 | 2 | 3 | 4 |

| 5) | sounds | 1 | 2 | 3 | 4 |

 **Write and read.**

6) _____

 **Choose the correct answer.**

7) What is the syllable type?
   - ○ r-controlled
   - ○ closed
   - ○ open

Listen!

? Circle the correct answers.

| 8) | syllables | 1 | 2 | 3 | 4 |

| 9) | sounds | 1 | 2 | 3 | 4 |

 **Write and read.**

10) _____

? Choose the correct answer.

11) The vowel sound is ____.
   - ○ short
   - ○ long
   - ○ r-controlled

Listen!

 **Circle the correct answers.**

12) | syllables | 1 2 3 4 |

13) | sounds | 1 2 3 4 |

 **Write and read.**

14) _____

 **Choose the correct answer.**

15) What is the syllable type?
- ○ closed
- ○ open
- ○ r-controlled

Choose the correct answers.

16) Mark (☒) TWO words that end with a consonant sound.

☐ her

☐ burn

☐ hurt

Write the correct answers.
Complete the sentences.

her	burn	hurt

17) Tyler got _____ when he fell off the monkey bars.

18) If you wait for the soup to cool, it will not _____ you.

19) I gave my mom a card for _____ birthday.

SCORE   CORRECT   RESCORE

Learn:

- Divide and read words with r-controlled vowels.

- Spell and read words from List 7.

WRITING PHONOGRAM REVIEW

 **Listen to and write the correct phonograms.**
Underline any multi-letter phonograms.

WORKING WITH WORDS

The words in this Lesson have the r-controlled vowels **ar** and **or**.

 **Divide and read the words.**
Circle the picture that shows each word.

1) target

2) garden

3) party

4) forty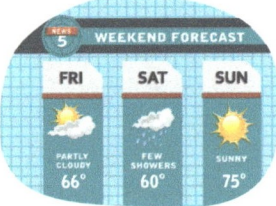

5) acorn

Listen!

 **Circle the correct answers.**

| 6) | syllables | 1 | 2 | 3 | 4 |

| 7) | sounds | 1 | 2 | 3 | 4 |

 **Write and read.**

8) _____

 **Choose the correct answer.**

9) What is the syllable type?
   - ○ closed
   - ○ open
   - ○ r-controlled

Listen!

Circle the correct answers.

| 10) | syllables | 1 | 2 | 3 | 4 |

| 11) | sounds | 1 | 2 | 3 | 4 |

Write and read.

12) _____

Choose the correct answer.

13) What is the syllable type?
   ○ r-controlled
   ○ VCe
   ○ vowel team

Listen!

 **Circle the correct answers.**

14) | syllables | 1 | 2 | 3 | 4 |

15) | sounds | 1 | 2 | 3 | 4 |

 **Write and read.**

16) _____

 **Choose the correct answer.**

17) The vowel sound is ____.
   ○ short
   ○ r-controlled
   ○ long

Listen!

 **Circle the correct answers.**

| 18) | syllables | 1 | 2 | 3 | 4 |

| 19) | sounds | 1 | 2 | 3 | 4 |

 **Write and read.**

20) _____

 **Choose the correct answer.**

21) Which reading rule does this word follow?
   - ○ **o** before **m**, **n**, or **v**
   - ○ middle **s**
   - ○ 1st sound of **c**

? Choose the correct answers.

22) Mark (☒) TWO words that have the same vowel sound.

☐ for   ☐ born   ☐ car

✏ Write the correct answers.
Sort the words in ABC order.

part	born	for

23) _____

24) _____

25) _____

✏ Use the word in your own sentence.

car

26) _____

SCORE   CORRECT   RESCORE

ACTIVITY: R-controlled Nonsense Words

You can read and spell r-controlled syllables.
Now read these nonsense words.

merp	dirb	terf	zarp	forp
serk	mir	nurch	quarf	borx
purk	birt	lur	darb	morp
ferb	tirth	gurk	sarph	orl
erp	mirp	urnk	zarsh	torb
flerx	quirl	darf	torp	virk

Learn:

- Divide and read two-syllable words.

- Spell and read words from List 7.

WRITING PHONOGRAM REVIEW

Listen to and write the phonograms.
Underline any multi-letter phonograms.

WORKING WITH WORDS

Sometimes, VCCV words divide after the first vowel. This can happen when the letter **r** is the second consonant. It can take the first consonant with it.

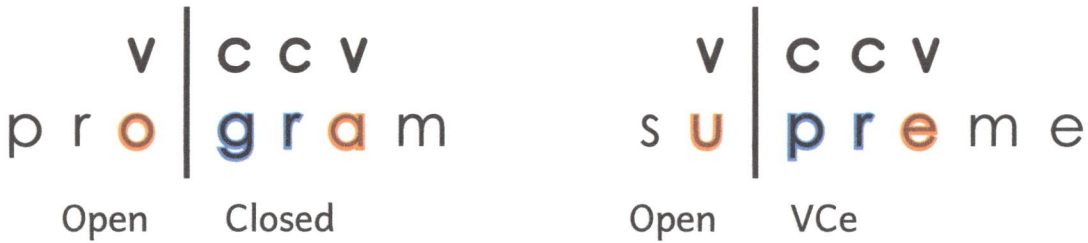

v	c c v		v	c c v	
p r **o**	**g r a** m		s **u**	**p r e** m e	
Open	Closed		Open	VCe	

Divide and read the words.
Remember, underline the multi-letter phonograms first.

secret	April	migrate	sacred
micro	zebra	vibrate	cobra
rubric	agree	across	matrix

Listen!

Circle the correct answers.

1) syllables   1   2   3   4

2) sounds   1   2   3   4

Write and read.

3) _____

Choose the correct answer.

4) What is the syllable type?
   - ○ vowel team
   - ○ open
   - ○ r-controlled

Listen!

 **Circle the correct answers.**

| 5) | syllables | 1 | 2 | 3 | 4 |

| 6) | sounds | 1 | 2 | 3 | 4 |

✏️ **Write and read.**

7) _____

❓ **Choose the correct answer.**

8) The vowel sound is ____.
   ○ r-controlled
   ○ short
   ○ long

Listen!

? **Circle the correct answers.**

| 9) | syllables | 1 | 2 | 3 | 4 |

| 10) | sounds | 1 | 2 | 3 | 4 |

✏️ **Write and read.**

11) _____

? **Choose the correct answer.**

12) Which reading rule does this word follow?

○ beginning **s**

○ **o** before **m**, **n**, or **v**

○ 1st sound of **c**

13) **Stir** the milk to mix it with the cocoa.

14) Irwin is digging a hole in the **dirt**.

15) The **girl** has a red bookmark.

SCORE   CORRECT   RESCORE

PHONOGRAM REVIEW

 **Listen to and circle the correct phonograms.**

1)    oy   oi   ow

2)    ou   ough   ow

3)    p   qu   j

4)    ough   ee   oo

5)    tch   th   ck

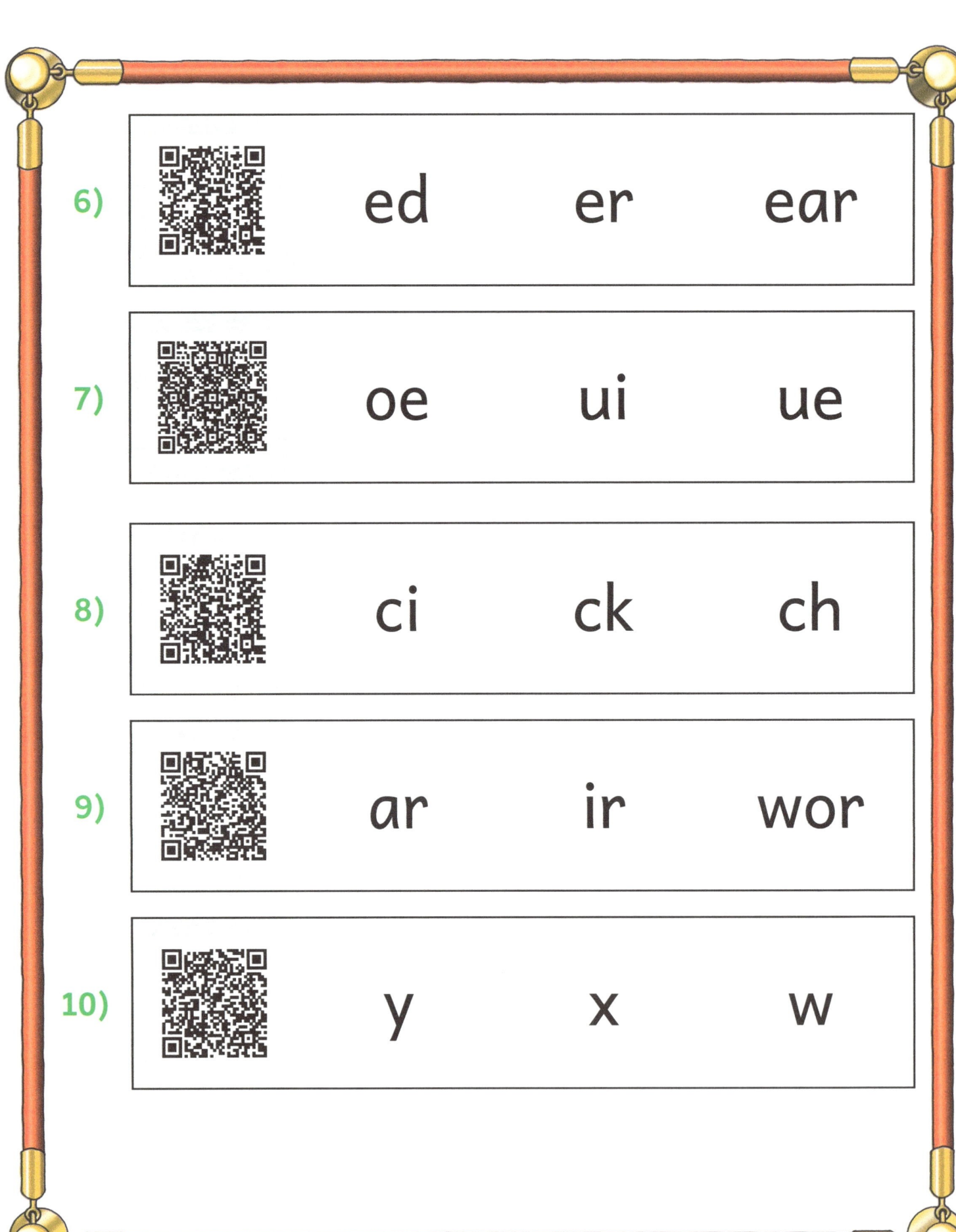

6)   ed   er   ear

7)   oe   ui   ue

8)   ci   ck   ch

9)   ar   ir   wor

10)   y   x   w

11)		r	wor	n
12)		ck	kn	k
13)		w	v	p
14)		oy	ey	ea
15)		oe	eigh	oa

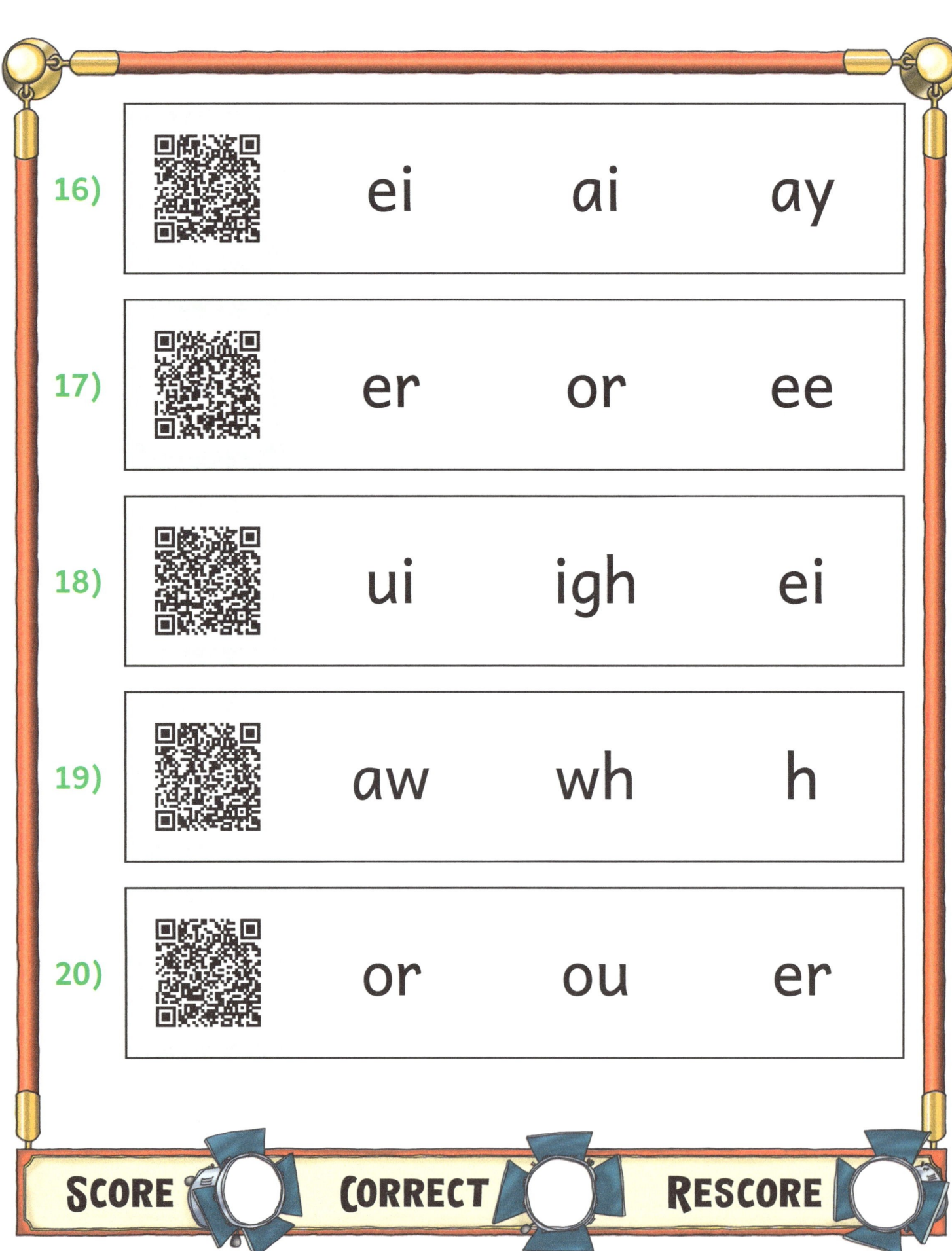

16) ei   ai   ay

17) er   or   ee

18) ui   igh   ei

19) aw   wh   h

20) or   ou   er

SPELLING LIST 7 REVIEW

✏️ **Write the correct answers.**
Read and sort the words by the position of the r-controlled vowel.

her	burn	hurt	for	born
part	car	dirt	girl	stir

1) **Middle**

2) **End**

This Reader has the tricky word *your*.
The letters **our** make the sound of **or**.

Tricky Word
your

))) **Listen to the forms of *your* in this sentence.**

If this game is **yours**, **you** need to put it in
your bag.

 **Write the correct answers.**
Complete the sentences.

you   your   yours

_____

1) He thinks this painting is mine, but I think it is _____.

_____

2) Did _____ make this painting?

_____

3) Is this _____ painting?

Reader 14
Circus Fun!

 **Choose the correct answers.**

4) What was in the tent?
- ○ a sleeping bag
- ○ a circus
- ○ a wedding

5) How did Pip get hurt?
- ○ He drove the beach car too fast.
- ○ Oat tried to jump over him.
- ○ He ate his hot dog when it was too hot.

6) What did Bix give Pip?
- ○ a cool drink
- ○ a bandage
- ○ a hot dog

Phonogram Test 19

Listen to and write the correct phonograms.
Underline any multi-letter phonograms.

1)

2)

3)

4)

5)

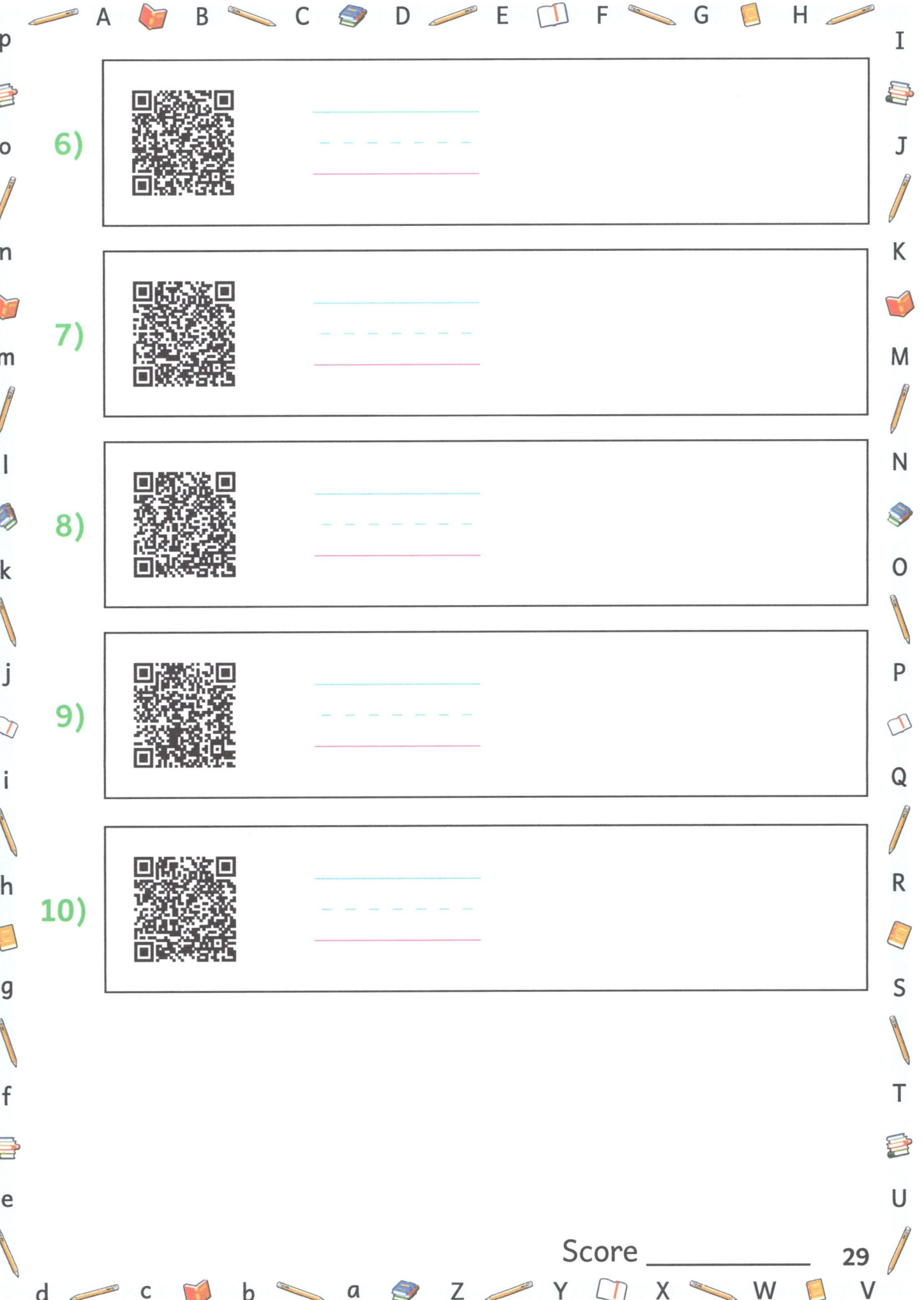

Spelling Test List 7

Listen to and write the spelling words.

1)

2)

3)

4)

5)

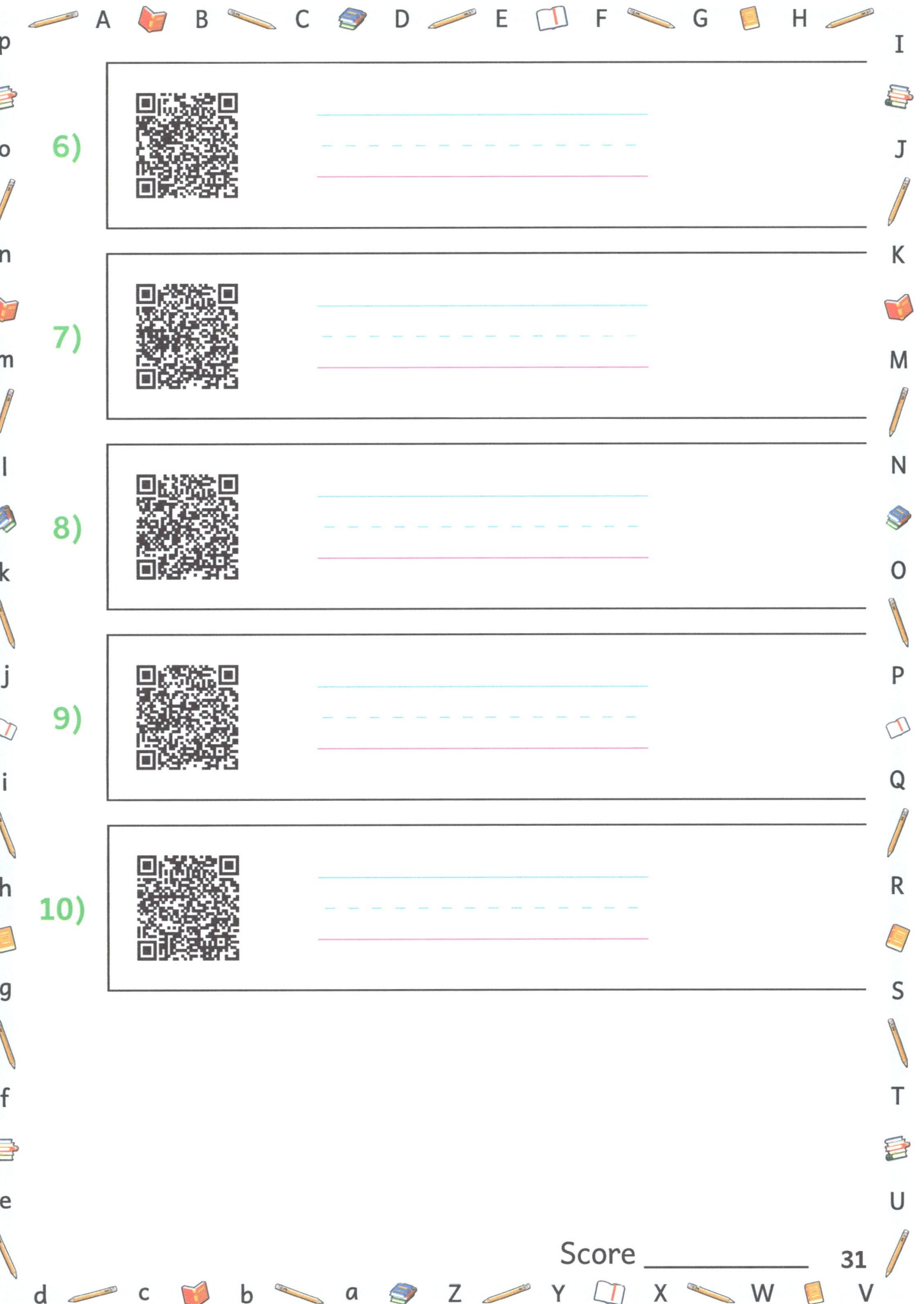

Learn:

- Divide and read two-syllable words with vowel teams.

- Spell and read words from List 8.

WRITING PHONOGRAM REVIEW

 **Listen to and write the phonograms.**
Underline any multi-letter phonograms.

WORKING WITH WORDS

Spelling List 8 has the vowel teams **oy**, **ow**, and **oi**.

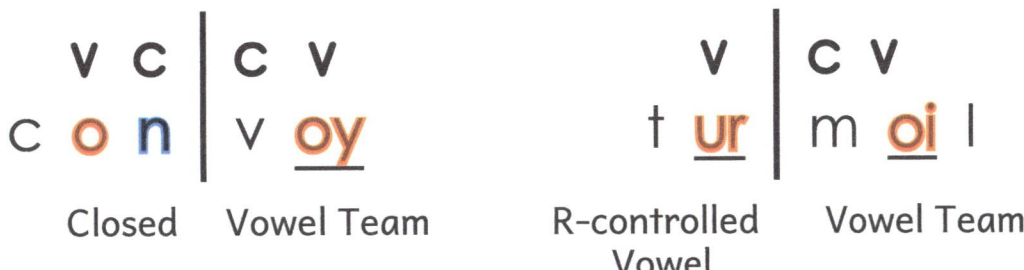

v c	c v		v	c v
c **o** n	v **oy**		t **ur**	m **oi** l
Closed	Vowel Team		R-controlled Vowel	Vowel Team

 **Mark, divide, and read the VCCV and VCV words.**
Remember, underline the multi-letter phonograms first.

decoy

oyster

sirloin

soymilk

yellow

tabloid

powder

window

33

Listen!

 **Circle the correct answers.**

1)	syllables	1	2	3	4

2)	sounds	1	2	3	4

 **Write and read.**

3) _____

 **Choose the correct answer.**

4) What is the syllable type?
   ○ vowel team
   ○ open
   ○ VCe

Listen!

 **Circle the correct answers.**

5)	syllables	1	2	3	4

6)	sounds	1	2	3	4

 **Write and read.**

7) _____

 **Choose the correct answer.**

8) What is the syllable type?
  ○ r-controlled
  ○ vowel team
  ○ open

? Circle the correct answer.

9)

syllables	1	2	3	4

? Circle the correct answers.
Then, write each syllable.

10)

syllable 1				
sounds	1	2	3	4

11)

syllable 2				
sounds	1	2	3	4

✏ Write and read.

12)

? Choose the correct answer.

13) Which word has two syllables?

○ boy   ○ toy   ○ enjoy

✏ Write the correct answers.
Complete the sentences.

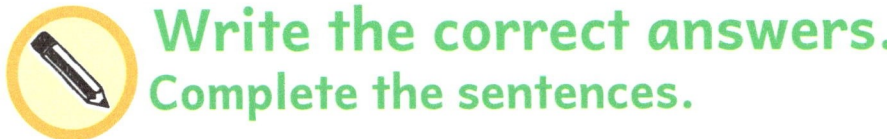

toy   boy   enjoy

14) Leroy and Boyd _____ making new pals.

15) Leroy asked the new _____ if he wanted to play.

16) Boyd showed him the _____ that makes silly sounds.

SCORE   CORRECT   RESCORE

5. SPELLING LIST 8: Part 2

Learn:

- Divide and read words with the VV division pattern.

- Spell and read words from List 8.

WRITING PHONOGRAM REVIEW

Listen to and write the phonograms.
Underline any multi-letter phonograms.

WORKING WITH WORDS

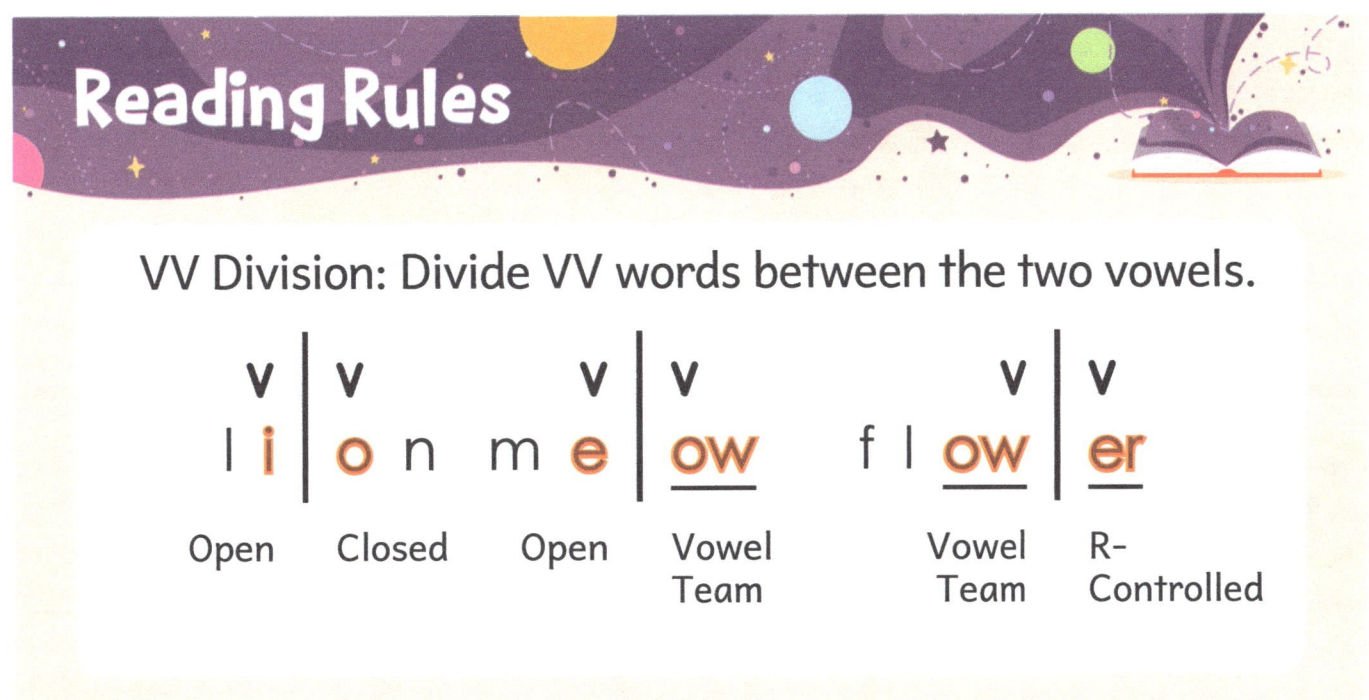

Reading Rules

VV Division: Divide VV words between the two vowels.

l i | o n m e | ow   f l ow | er

Open   Closed   Open   Vowel Team   Vowel Team   R-Controlled

Mark, divide, and read the VV words.
Remember, underline the multi-letter phonograms first.

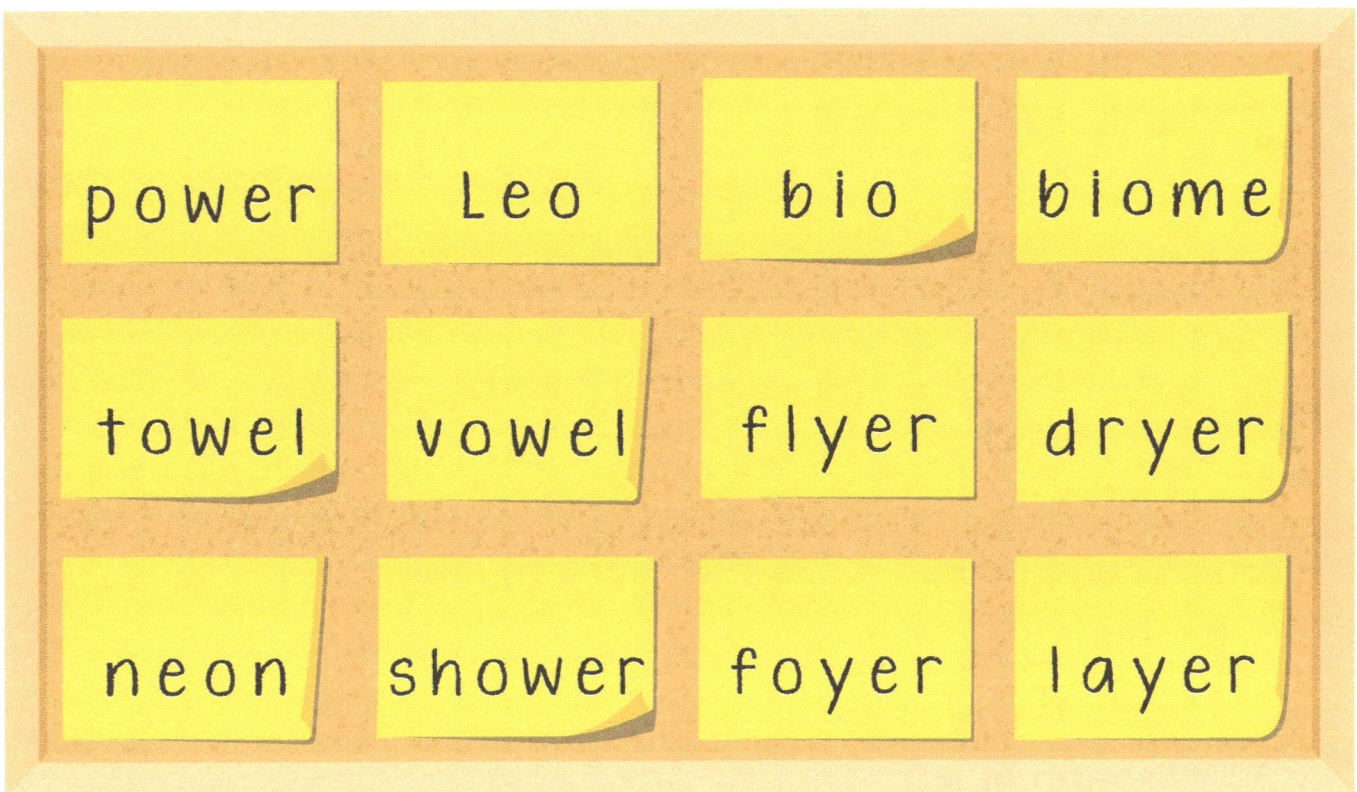

power	Leo	bio	biome
towel	vowel	flyer	dryer
neon	shower	foyer	layer

Listen!

 **Circle the correct answers.**

1) syllables   1   2   3   4

2) sounds   1   2   3   4

 **Write and read.**

3) _____

 **Choose the correct answer.**

4) Which reading rule does this word follow?
- ○ beginning **y**
- ○ 1st sound of **g**
- ○ 2nd sound of **g**

Listen!

? Circle the correct answers.

5) syllables	1	2	3	4

6) sounds	1	2	3	4

 **Write and read.**

7) _____

? Choose the correct answer.

8) What is the syllable type?
   - ○ vowel team
   - ○ open
   - ○ VCe

Listen!

 **Circle the correct answers.**

| 9) | syllables | 1 | 2 | 3 | 4 |

| 10) | sounds | 1 | 2 | 3 | 4 |

 **Write and read.**

11) _____

 **Choose the correct answer.**

12) How many consonant sounds are in the word?
- ○ 1
- ○ 2
- ○ 3

Listen!

? Circle the correct answers.

? Circle the correct answers.

13)

syllables	1	2	3	4

14)

sounds	1	2	3	4

✏️ **Write and read.**

15) _____

? Choose the correct answer.

16) What is the syllable type?
- ○ VCe
- ○ vowel team
- ○ r-controlled

 **Choose the correct answers.**

17) Mark (☒) TWO words that make the first sound of **ow**.

☐ down   ☐ blow   ☐ how

Write the correct answers.
Sort the words in ABC order.

how	blow	down

18) _____

19) _____

20) _____

Use the word in your own sentence.

grow

21) _____

SCORE	CORRECT	RESCORE

Learn:

- Divide and read words with the VCV and VV patterns.

- Spell and read words from List 8.

WRITING PHONOGRAM REVIEW

 **Listen to and write the phonograms.**
Underline any multi-letter phonograms.

WORKING WITH WORDS

v	v		v	c	v
s <u>ew</u>	<u>er</u>		d e	t <u>ai</u>	l
Vowel Team	R-controlled vowel		Open	Vowel Team	

Mark, divide, and read the VCV and VV words.
Remember, underline the multi-letter phonograms first.

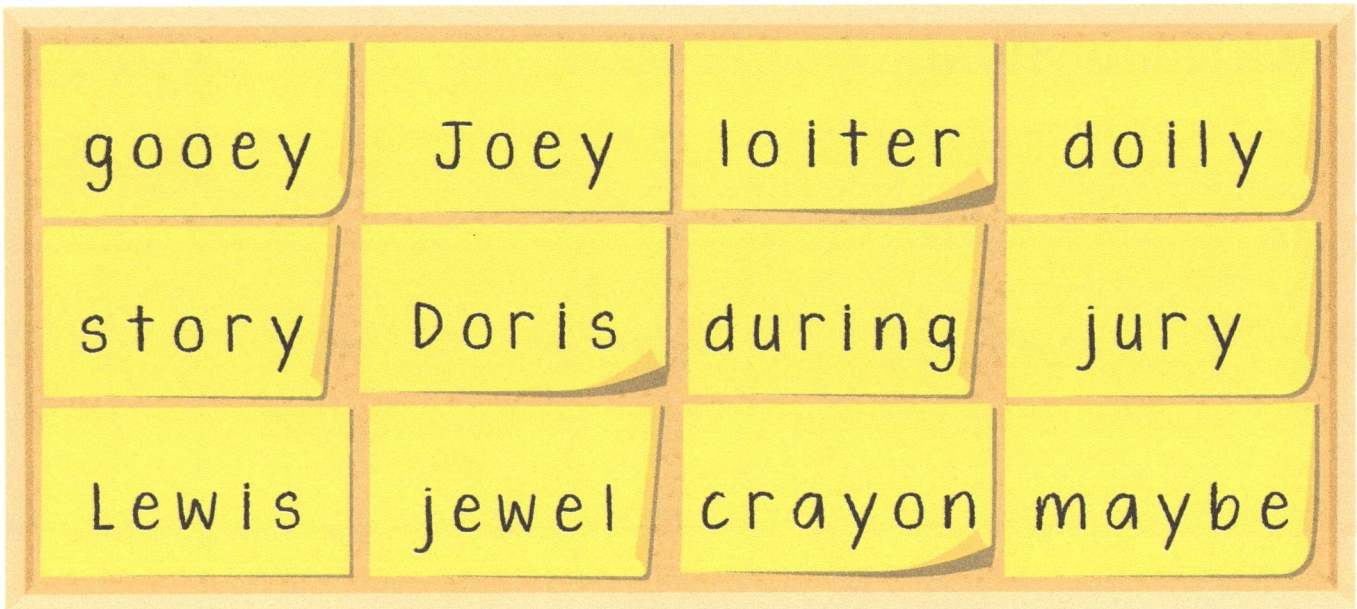

gooey	Joey	loiter	doily
story	Doris	during	jury
Lewis	jewel	crayon	maybe

46

Listen!

? **Circle the correct answers.**

1) syllables   1   2   3   4

2) sounds   1   2   3   4

✏ **Write and read.**

3) _____

? **Choose the correct answer.**

4) What is the syllable type?
   - ○ closed
   - ○ vowel team
   - ○ r-controlled

Listen!

Circle the correct answers.

| 5) | syllables | 1 | 2 | 3 | 4 |

| 6) | sounds | 1 | 2 | 3 | 4 |

Write and read.

7) _____

Choose the correct answer.

8) Which reading rule does this word follow?
- ○ beginning **s**
- ○ double **s**
- ○ 2nd sound of **c**

Listen!

(?) Circle the correct answers.

9) syllables   1   2   3   4

10) sounds   1   2   3   4

✏ Write and read.

11) _____

(?) Choose the correct answer.

12) Which reading rule does this word follow?
- ○ beginning **y**
- ○ 1ˢᵗ sound of **c**
- ○ 2ⁿᵈ sound of **c**

Circle the correct answers.
Which picture describes the sentence?

13) Lucy put the flowers in the **soil**.

14) This **coin** is shiny.

15) Many places cook fries in **oil**.

SCORE   CORRECT   RESCORE

PHONOGRAM REVIEW

 Listen to and circle the correct phonograms.

1) nk   ng   n

2)  nk   gn   kn

3)  aw   ai   au

4)  ou   ow   oe

5) tch   igh   eigh

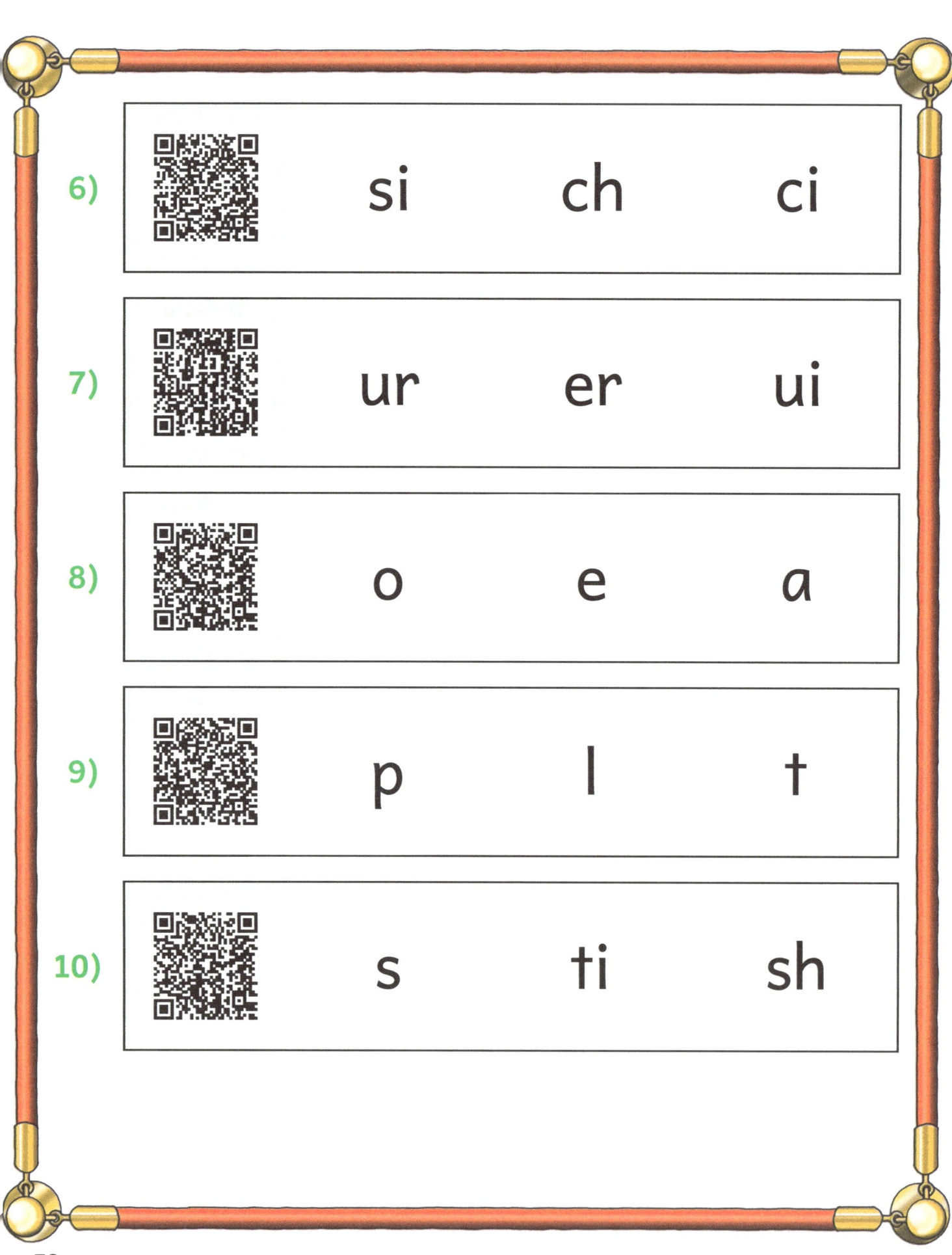

6) si ch ci

7) ur er ui

8) o e a

9) p l t

10) s ti sh

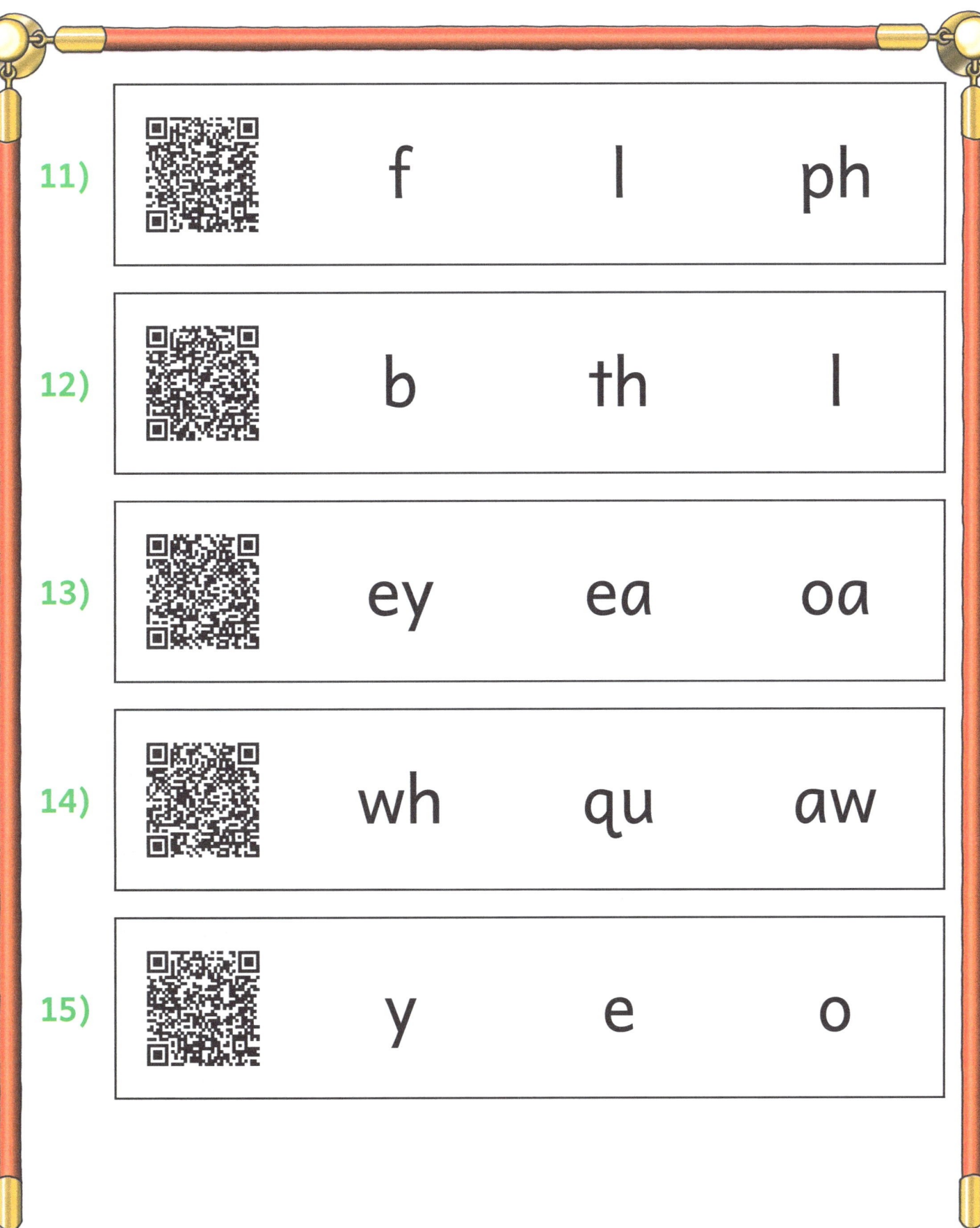

11) f   l   ph

12) b   th   l

13) ey   ea   oa

14) wh   qu   aw

15) y   e   o

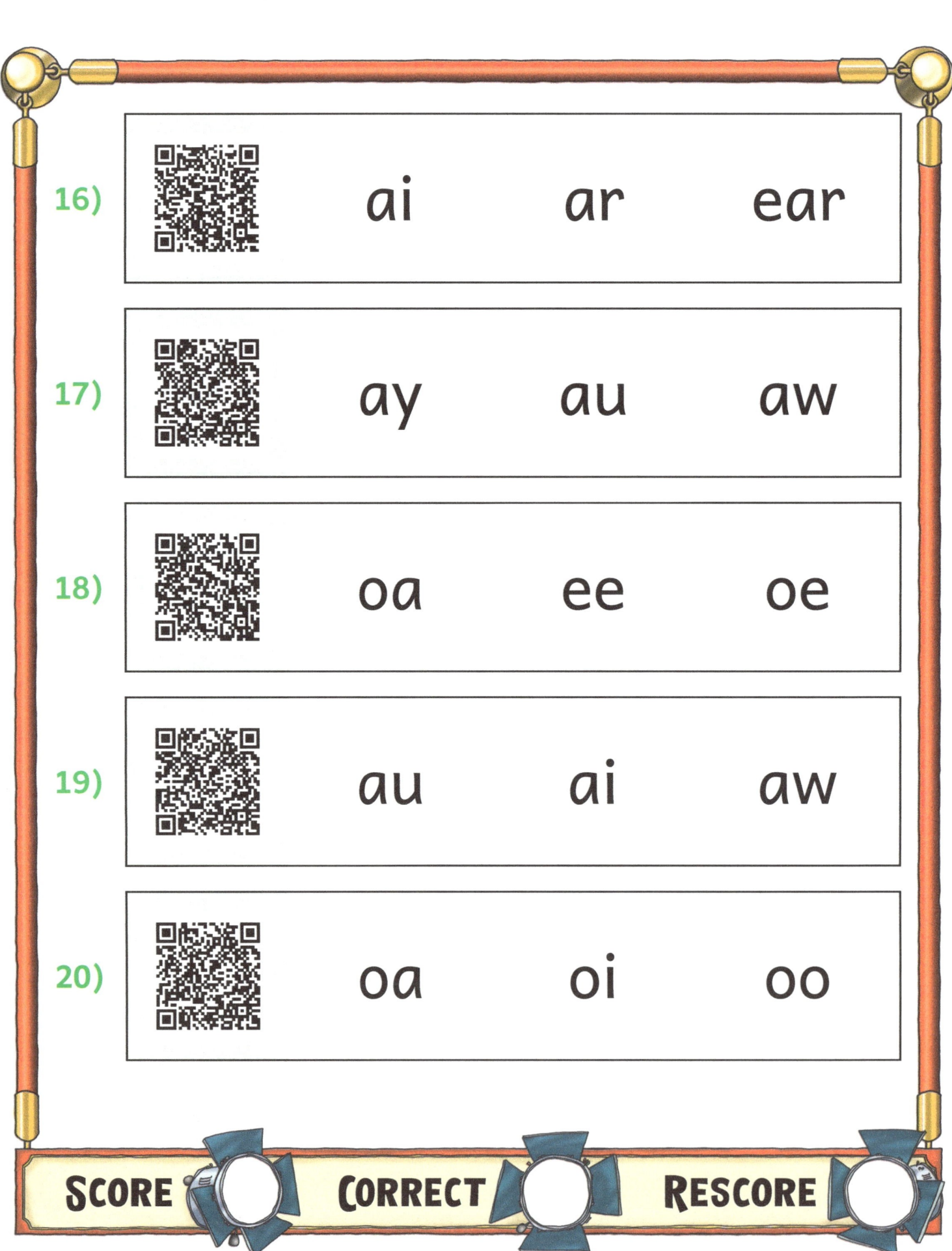

16) ai ar ear

17) ay au aw

18) oa ee oe

19) au ai aw

20) oa oi oo

SPELLING LIST 8 REVIEW

 **Write the correct answers.**
Sort the words under the correct pictures.

boy   toy   enjoy   grow   blow

down   how   oil   soil   coin

1)

2)

3)

4)

5)

6)

7)

8)

9)

10)

READER 15: "The Stormy Day"

This Reader has the tricky word *says*. The vowel team **ay** does not make its usual sound. It sounds like the short sound of **e**.

 **Listen to the word *says* in this sentence.**

The sign **says**, "Do not walk on the grass."

 **Choose the correct answer.**

1) What do you think this card says inside?
   - ○ "Good luck!"
   - ○ "Happy Birthday!"
   - ○ "Thank you!"

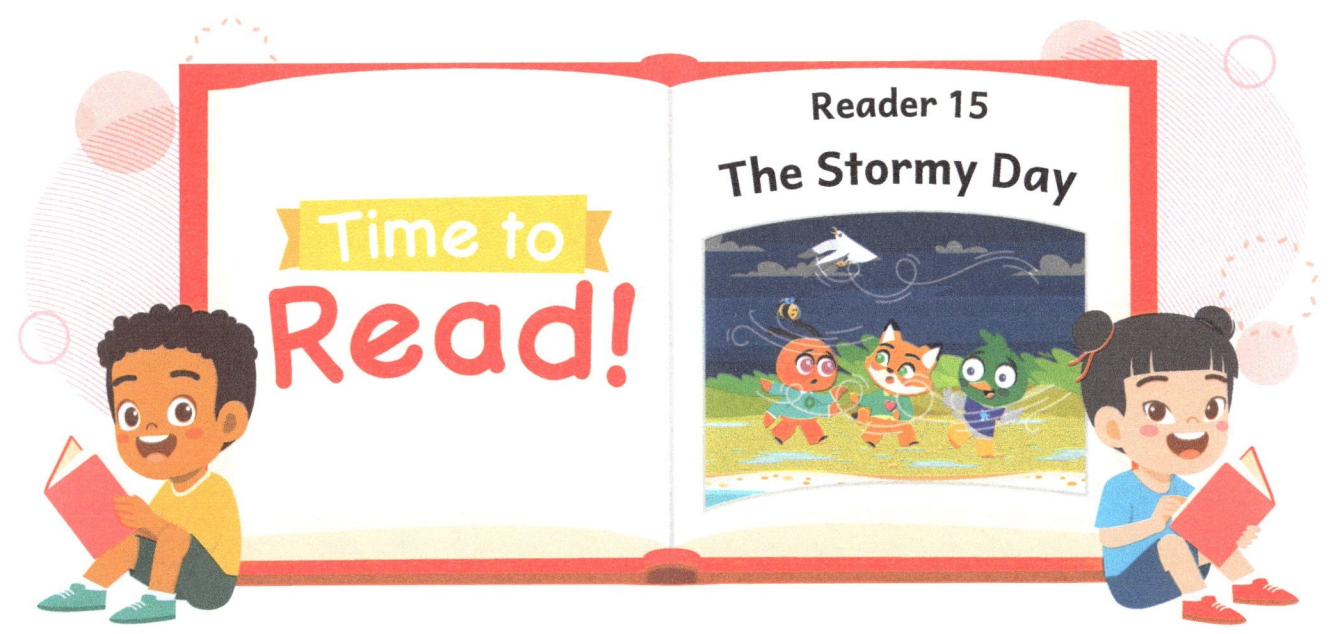

Reader 15

The Stormy Day

 **Choose the correct answers.**

2) Why did the pals go to the beach?
   - ○ to help clean up
   - ○ to swim in the water
   - ○ to have a picnic

3) What did Zip pick up?
   - ○ a plant
   - ○ a laptop
   - ○ a toy

4) How did the pals get through the strong wind?
   - ○ They ran back home.
   - ○ They jumped in the water.
   - ○ They held hands.

Phonogram Test 20

Listen to and write the correct phonograms.
Underline any multi-letter phonograms.

1)

2)

3)

4)

5)

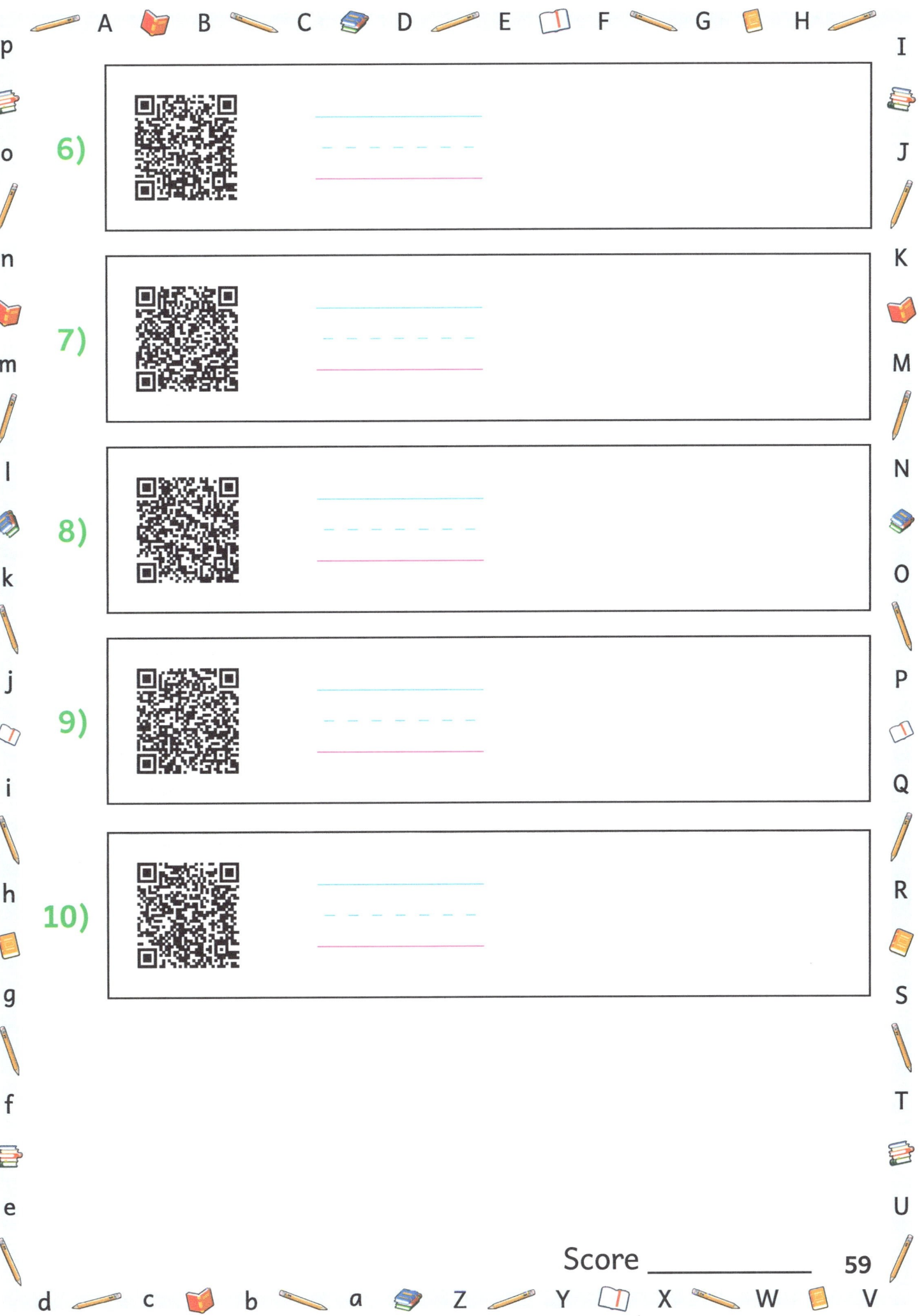

Spelling Test List 8

Listen to and write the spelling words.

1)

2)

3)

4)

5)

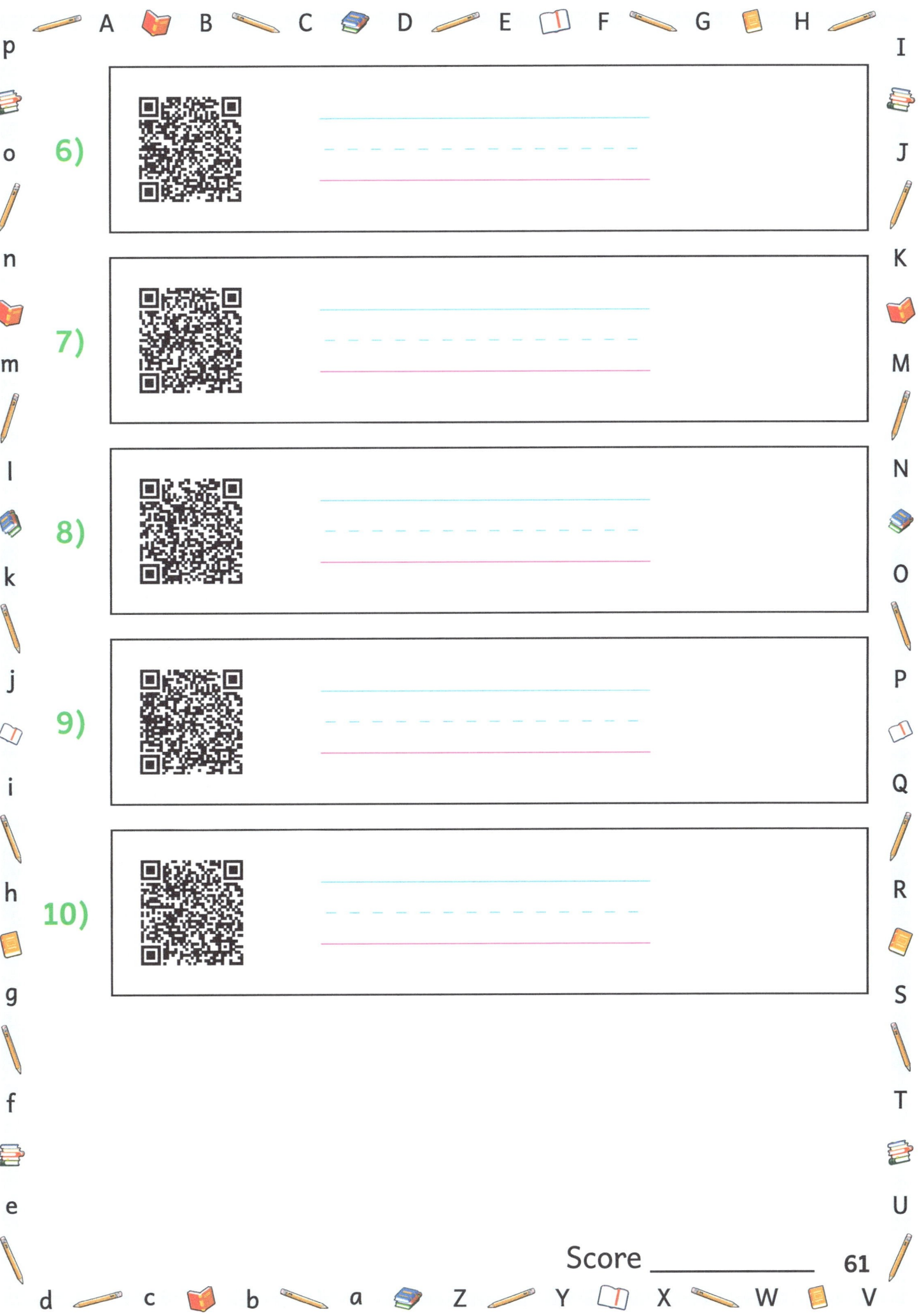

A　B　C　D　E　F　G　H

p　o　n　m　l　k　j　i　h　g　f　e　d

I　J　K　M　N　O　P　Q　R　S　T　U

c　b　a　Z　Y　X　W　V

6)

7)

8)

9)

10)

Learn:

- Read tricky words with vowel teams **ou** and **ai**.

- Spell and read words from List 9.

WRITING PHONOGRAM REVIEW

 **Listen to and write the phonograms.**
Underline any multi-letter phonograms.

WORKING WITH WORDS

Spelling List 9 has tricky words. This Lesson has vowel teams that do not make their usual sounds.

In a few words, the vowel team **ou** is r-controlled. The letters **our** say **or**.

p**our**   y**our**   c**our**t

Sometimes, the vowel team **ai** makes a lazy short **e** sound.

capt**ai**n   fount**ai**n   vill**ai**n

Write the correct answers.
Complete the sentences.

court	villain	your

1) Is this _____ book?

2) I found it on the tennis _____.

3) That fairy tale has a mean _____.

Listen!

 **Circle the correct answers.**

| 4) syllables | 1 | 2 | 3 | 4 |

| 5) sounds | 1 | 2 | 3 | 4 |

✏️ **Write and read.**

6) _____

❓ **Choose the correct answer.**

7) The vowel sound is ____.
- ○ short
- ○ long
- ○ r-controlled

Listen!

? **Circle the correct answers.**

8)
syllables	1	2	3	4

9)
sounds	1	2	3	4

✏️ **Write and read.**

10) _____

? **Choose the correct answer.**

11) Which reading rule does this word follow?
- ○ beginning **s**
- ○ 1ˢᵗ sound of **g**
- ○ 2ⁿᵈ sound of **g**

Listen!

Circle the correct answer.

12) | syllables | **1** | **2** | **3** | **4** |

Circle the correct answers.
Then, write each syllable.

13) syllable 1

sounds 1 2 3 4

_____

14) syllable 2

sounds 1 2 3 4

_____

Write and read.

15) _____

 **Choose the correct answers.**

16) Which word means to repeat something?
- ○ four
- ○ again
- ○ said

17) Which word is a number?
- ○ four
- ○ again
- ○ said

18) Which word is the past tense of *say*?
- ○ four
- ○ again
- ○ said

SCORE ○ CORRECT ○ RESCORE ○

Learn:

- Read words with silent letters.

- Spell and read words from List 9.

WRITING PHONOGRAM REVIEW

 ## Listen to and write the phonograms.
Underline any multi-letter phonograms.

WORKING WITH WORDS
This Lesson has words with silent letters.

knight   pa**l**ms   s**w**ord

Circle the correct answers.

1) Which TWO words begin with the same sound?

| knee | calf | wrist | nose |

2) Which TWO words rhyme?

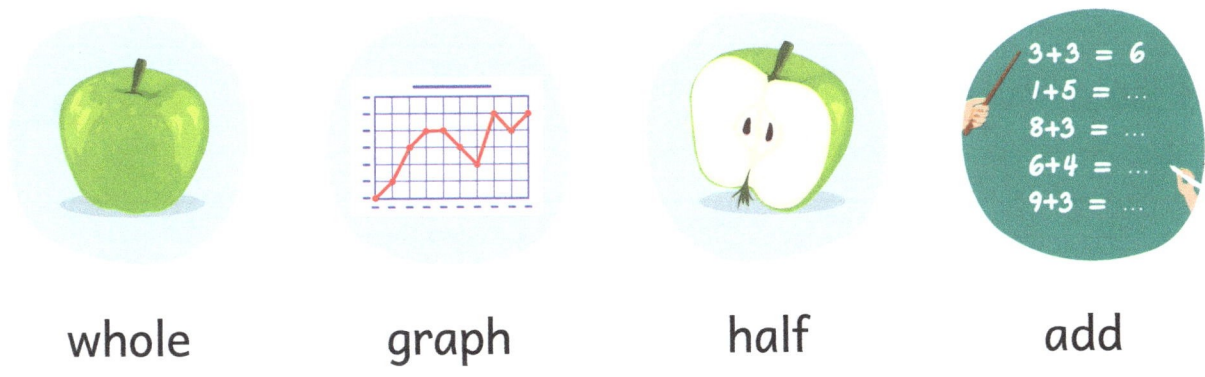

| whole | graph | half | add |

3) Which TWO words have all the same sounds?

| white | light | write | right |

Listen!

Circle the correct answers.

4) | syllables | 1 | 2 | 3 | 4 |

5) | sounds | 1 | 2 | 3 | 4 |

Write and read.

6) _____

Choose the correct answer.

7) Which letter is silent?
- ○ c
- ○ l
- ○ d

Listen!

? Circle the correct answers.

8) syllables   1   2   3   4

9) sounds   1   2   3   4

✏ Write and read.

10) _____

? Choose the correct answer.

11) Which letter is silent?
 ○ w
 ○ d
 ○ l

Listen!

❓ Circle the correct answers.

12)

| syllables | 1 | 2 | 3 | 4 |

13)

| sounds | 1 | 2 | 3 | 4 |

✏️ Write and read.

14) _____

❓ Choose the correct answer.

15) Which letter is silent?
   ○ k
   ○ o
   ○ n

Listen!

? Circle the correct answers.

16)	syllables	1	2	3	4

17)	sounds	1	2	3	4

✏ Write and read.

18) _____

? Choose the correct answer.

19) Which letter is silent?
   - ○ t
   - ○ w
   - ○ o

❓ Choose the correct answers.

20) Mark (☒) TWO words that rhyme.

☐ two ☐ would ☐ could

✏️ Write the correct answers.
Sort the words in ABC order.

would	could	two

21) _____

22) _____

23) _____

✏️ Use the word in your own sentence.

know

24) _____

SCORE   CORRECT   RESCORE

76

Learn:

- Read words with the long **i** and **o** sounds before two consonants.

- Spell and read words from List 9.

WRITING PHONOGRAM REVIEW

Listen to and write the phonograms.
Underline any multi-letter phonograms.

WORKING WITH WORDS

Reading Rules

Long **i** and **o** before two consonants: The letters **i** and **o** often make their long sounds when they come before two consonants.

w**i**ld   c**o**lt

Write the correct answers.
Sort the words under the correct pictures.

child   gold   blinds   r oll

1)

2)

3)

4)

_____

_____

_____

Listen!

 **Circle the correct answers.**

5)	syllables	1	2	3	4

6)	sounds	1	2	3	4

 **Write and read.**

7) _____

 **Choose the correct answer.**

8) The vowel sound is ____.
   - ○ short
   - ○ long
   - ○ r-controlled

Listen!

Circle the correct answers.

9)	syllables	1	2	3	4

10)	sounds	1	2	3	4

Write and read.

11) _____

Choose the correct answer.

12) The vowel sound is ____.
   ○ short
   ○ r–controlled
   ○ long

Listen!

? **Circle the correct answers.**

13) | syllables | 1 2 3 4

14) | sounds | 1 2 3 4

✏️ **Write and read.**

15) _____

? **Choose the correct answer.**

16) Which reading rule does this word follow?
- ○ long **o** before two consonants
- ○ **o** before **m**, **n**, or **v**
- ○ 1ˢᵗ sound of **c**

81

❓ Choose the correct answers.

17) Mark (☒) TWO words that begin with the same sound.

☐ fold ☐ from ☐ both

✏️ Write the correct answers.
Complete the sentences.

from	both	fold

18) My teacher can _____ paper into shapes.

19) He used _____ red and green paper to make that rose.

20) He learned how to do it _____ his mom.

SCORE   CORRECT   RESCORE

PHONOGRAM REVIEW

 **Listen to and circle the correct phonograms.**

1)    ai   eigh   au

2)    ue   ea   ie

3)    aw   ay   au

4)    sh   ei   si

5)    ear   wor   or

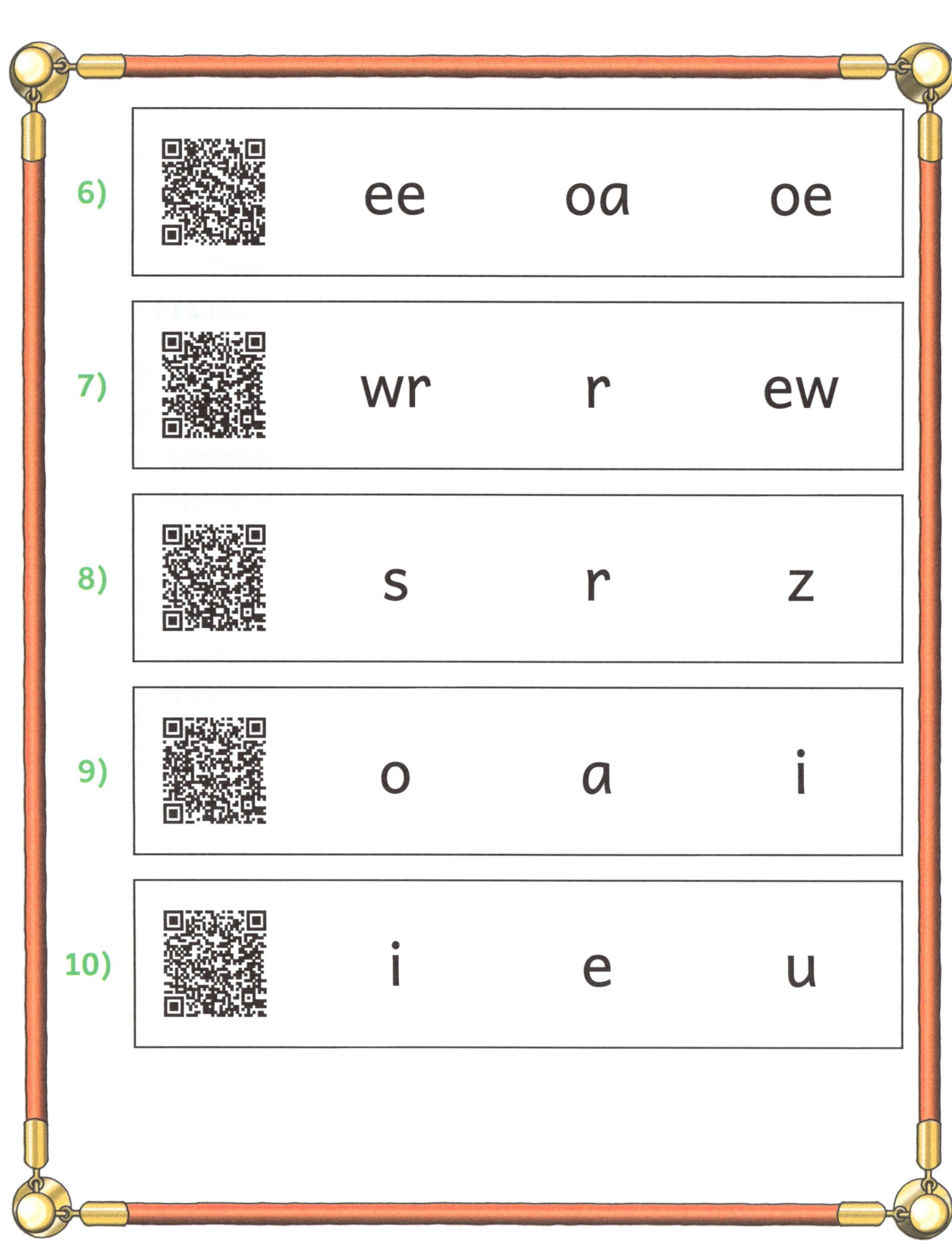

6) ee   oa   oe

7) wr   r   ew

8) s   r   z

9) o   a   i

10) i   e   u

11)	igh	i	ei
12)	ear	oa	ea
13)	ch	th	wh
14)	l	th	t
15)	g	j	p

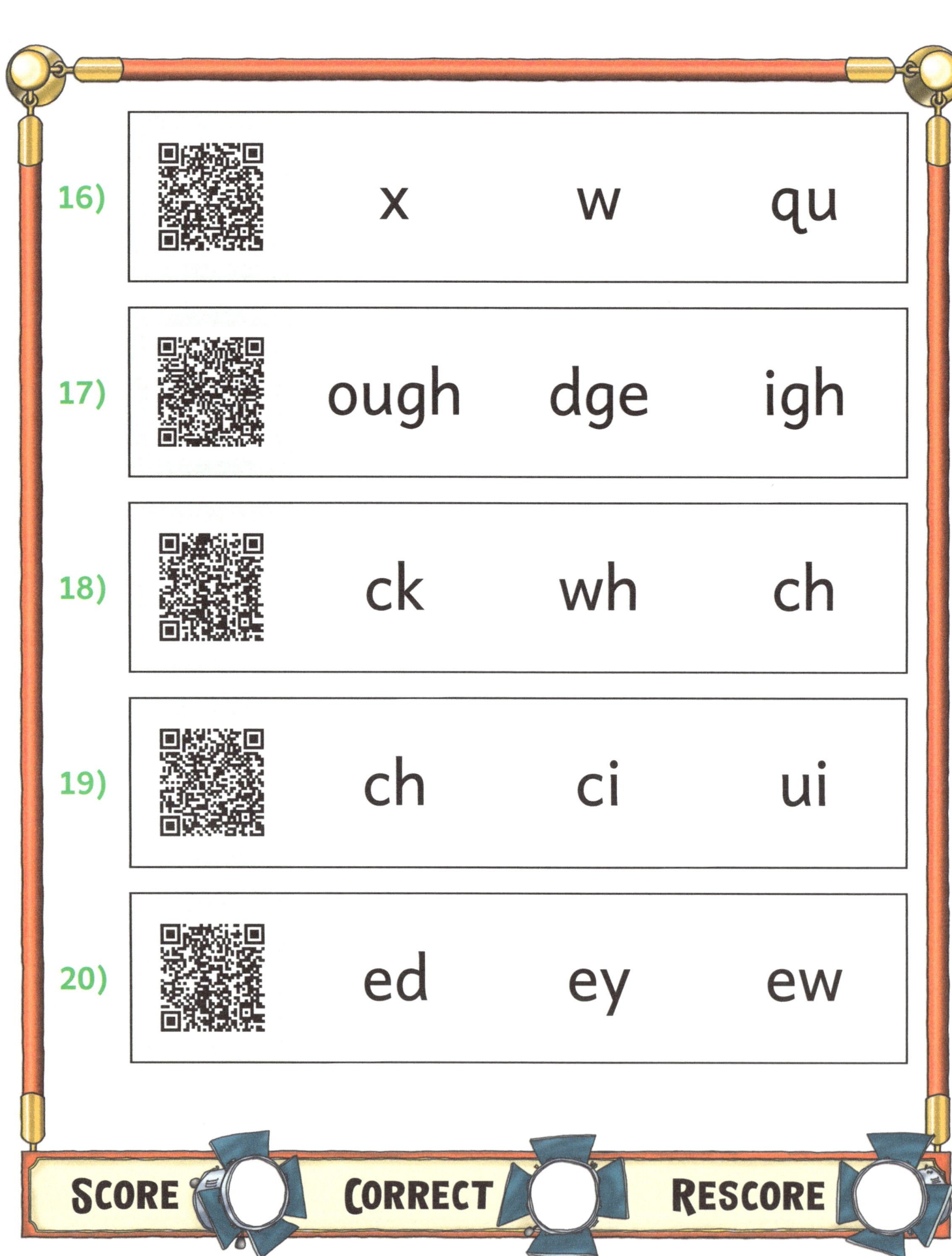

16) x   w   qu

17) ough   dge   igh

18) ck   wh   ch

19) ch   ci   ui

20) ed   ey   ew

SCORE   CORRECT   RESCORE

SPELLING LIST 9 REVIEW

 **Listen to and circle the correct words.**

1)  could   would   said

2)  fold   know   both

3)  again   said   from

4)  know   would   could

5)  from   four   fold

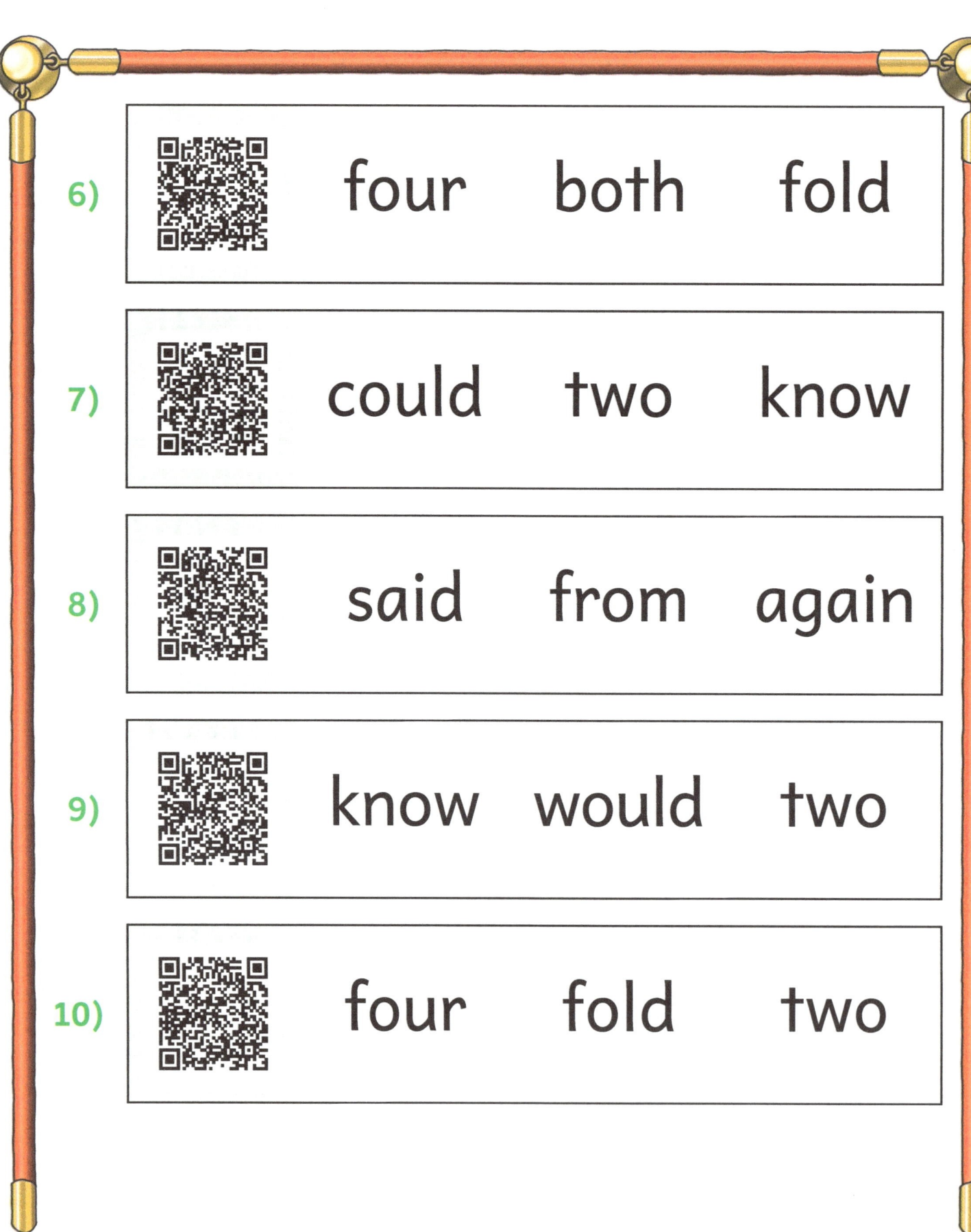

6) four   both   fold

7) could   two   know

8) said   from   again

9) know   would   two

10) four   fold   two

READER 16: "Beach Party"

Before you read, practice these words.

Read	Trace	Read	Trace
1) from	from	7) both	both
2) of	of	8) fold	fold
3) was	was	9) said	said
4) your	your	10) again	again
5) four	four	11) could	could
6) know	know	12) would	would

Time to Read!

Reader 16

Beach Party

 **Order from 1–3.**

Put the events in order.

13) _____ Kit cooks dinner.

_____ The pals sat by the fire.

_____ Kit invites Bix and Pip to a party.

 **Choose the correct answers.**

14) Who threw the party?
- O Pip
- O Bix
- O Kit

15) Who rode a bike?
- O Pip
- O Bix
- O Kit

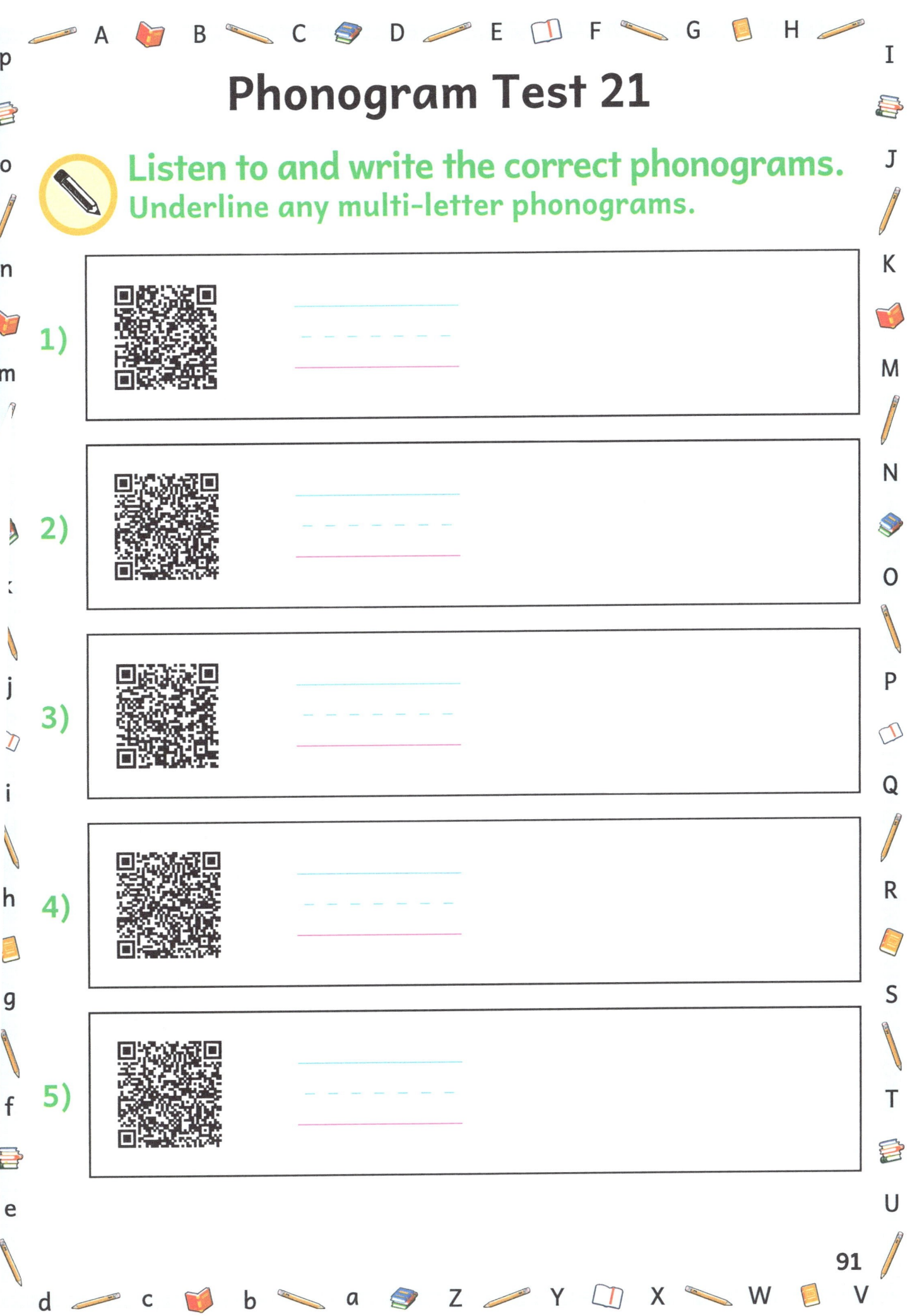

Phonogram Test 21

Listen to and write the correct phonograms.
Underline any multi-letter phonograms.

1)

2)

3)

4)

5)

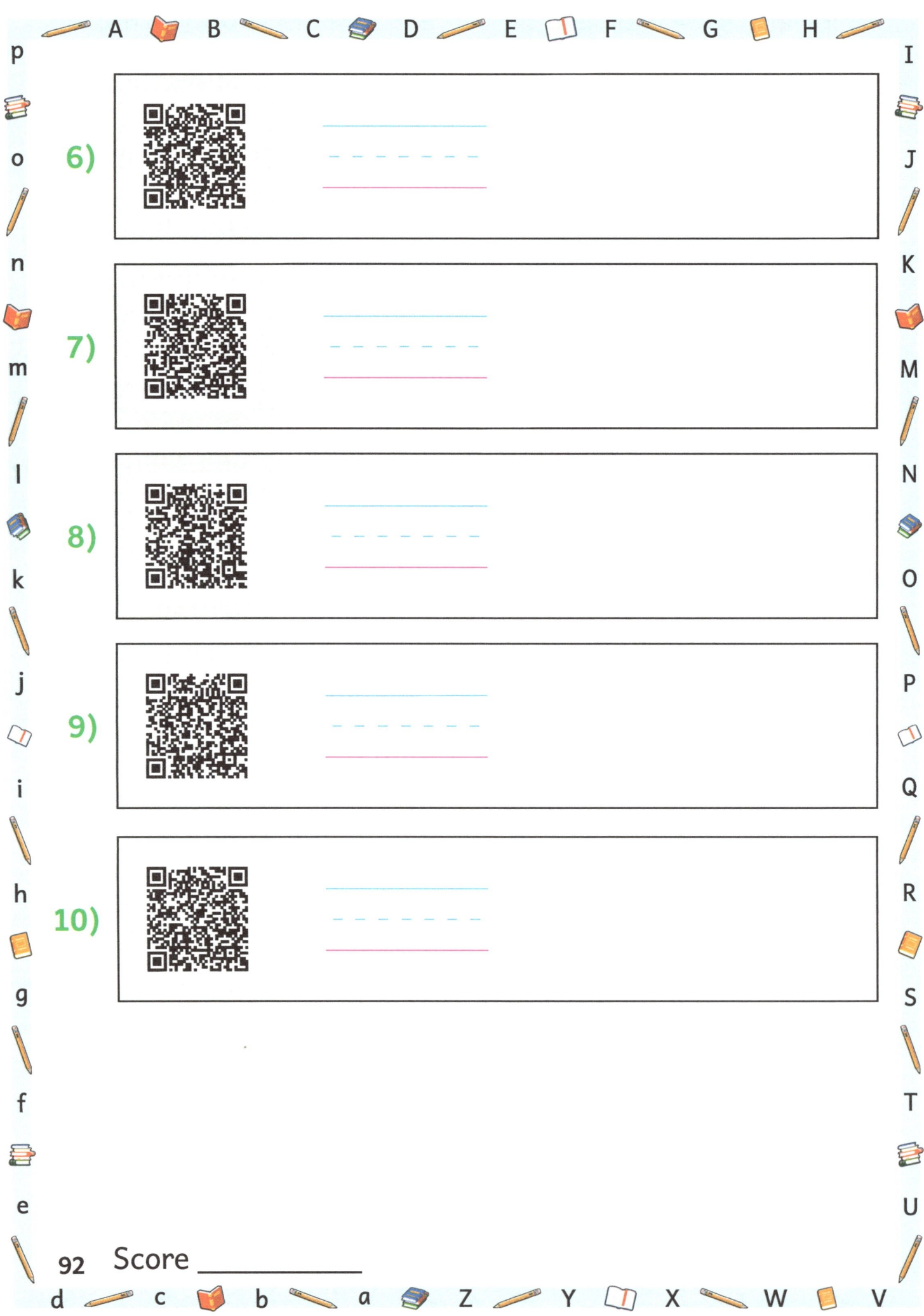

Score _____

Spelling Test List 9

Listen to and write the spelling words.

1)

2)

3)

4)

5)

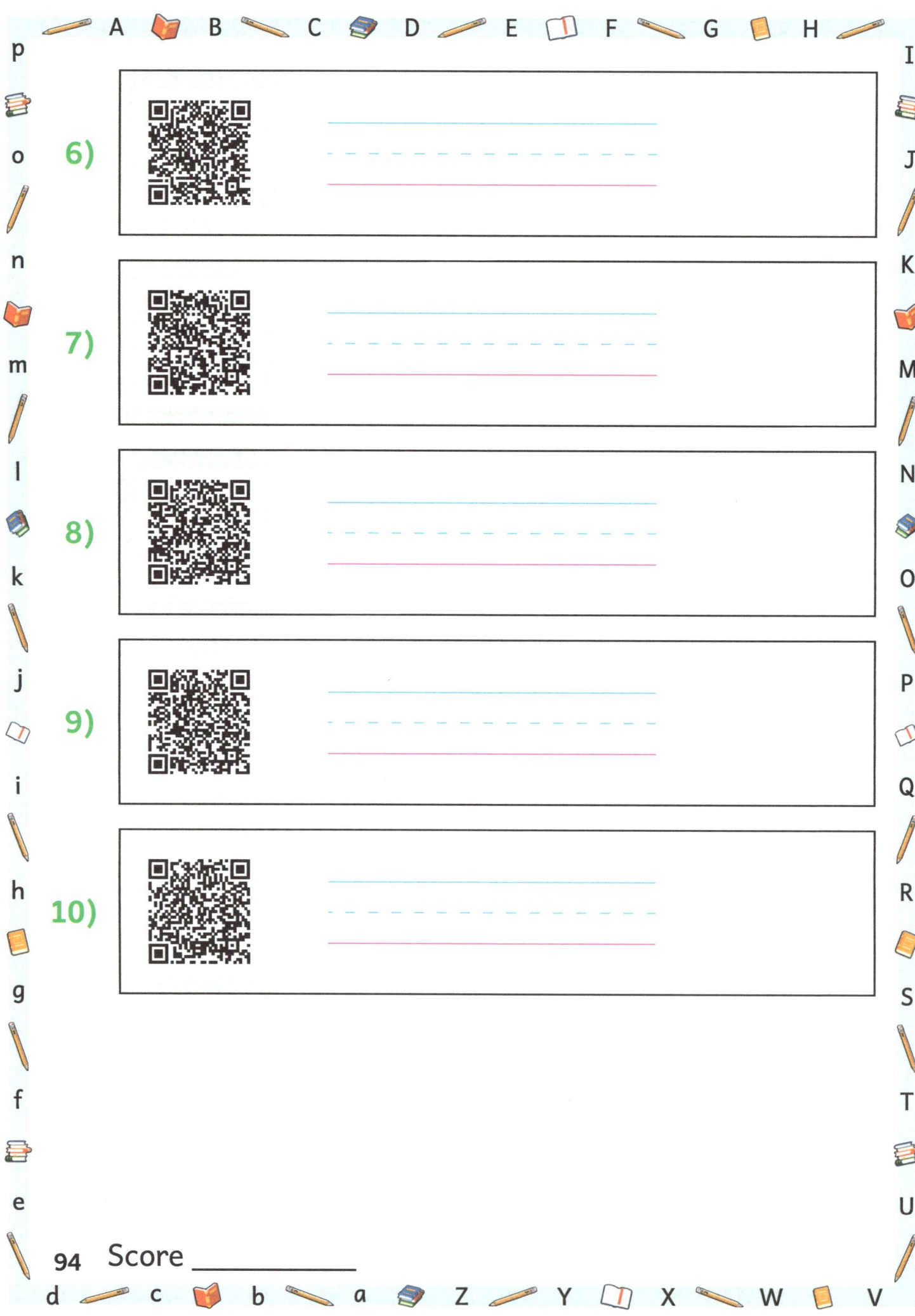

A B C D E F G H

p
o
n
m
l
k
j
i
h
g
f
e

6)

7)

8)

9)

10)

I
J
K
M
N
O
P
Q
R
S
T
U

94 Score _____

d c b a Z Y X W V